Gratitude Greens

An Intentional Feast in a Starving World

By

AD Masters

CROSSLINK
PUBLISHING

Gratitude Greens: An Intentional Feast in a Starving World

Ɖ CrossLink Publishing
Ȼ www.crosslinkpublishing.com

ISBN 978-0-9852896-1-4

Library of Congress Control Number: 2014931426

TABLE OF CONTENTS

PREFACE

Throughout my forty-plus years on this earth, I have endeavored to stay positive and be a light in the darkness. I have longed to be called a "Godly Woman," and yet I struggle to see myself as one. Sometimes I have a tendency to focus on lack and, therefore, bring down myself and those closest to me. However, I fully believe God has called me to lift my eyes to Heaven and see Him clearly in all His glory. He then calls me to walk closely beside Him and allow Him to shine His glory light through me. It's not up to me to *make* it happen; it's up to me to *let* it happen.

I am an avid reader and have gleaned much encouragement from Christian authors such as Angela Thomas, Beth Moore, and many others. After many years of keeping a personal journal as well as a gratitude journal, I began to realize how cathartic the writing process is for me. Then several years ago, I read Robin McGraw's first book, *Inside My Heart*, which she wrote at the age of fifty-two. It suddenly dawned on me that I wanted to be a writer. If she can do it at age fifty-two, surely I can write a book at age forty. I was scared, excited, doubtful, certain and giddy about the prospect of writing my first book.

However, I have been encouraged by so many Godly men and women over the years. My mom and dad have never ceased to cheer me on and inspire me to be the best "me" I can possibly be. My husband has been my biggest cheerleader, urging me to keep moving forward and reminding me to believe in myself and in the abilities God has blessed me with. He has praised me, roused me, and reassured me as needed. He has believed in me and reminded me that God believes in me, too. My wonderful editor and good friend, Mary, has reassured and emboldened me to push forward and believe in myself.

I have divided this book into two parts. Part 1 is comprised of several chapters that I hope will embolden you and give you a desire to make gratitude part of your daily life. Part 2 includes thirty days of devotionals and is meant to be read one day at a time. Each day, I included at least one scripture that I hope you will use as a springboard to a more thorough reading of the Word.

"Gratitude Greens" is a compilation of the encouragement I have received, the life experiences I have had, and the abilities and insights God has impressed upon me. This book is my gift to you, and my prayer is that it will offer you hope and purpose and will open your eyes to the many ways God is calling you to be used in His Story.

God Bless You!
-AD Masters

CHAPTER 1—INTRODUCTION

I love the color green. To me, it signifies freedom, wide open fields, cool grass between my toes on a warm summer evening. I can close my eyes and almost smell the color. Granny Smith Apple Green, Crayola calls it. Doesn't that just sound happy?

Others equate the color green with envy or anger. Pea green, dark forest green, green with envy. For me, this only happens when the grass is dry and browned, the forest is dark and foreboding, and the sun has gone behind the clouds. Someone has forgotten to water the fields. They have failed to nourish the soil and somehow blocked out the rays of sunshine from their days.

How can one color elicit and represent such different emotions? How can one person feel bubbles of joy popping up when he or she experiences green and another go down into the depths of heaviness? Colors can represent our views of life, how we see the world, the lenses we look through. Most people have many different lenses they look through, depending on their life circumstances or their moods.

We've all heard the saying "looking through rose-colored glasses." This is not usually meant as a compliment. It assumes naivety, denial, and lack of reality. That's sad to me. Why isn't it considered a positive quality to see life's good more than life's bad; to focus on the positive more than the negative? Why not look through gratitude-colored glasses: bright, happy green glasses through which all things work together for good?

I fully believe this is a choice that we each have. We live in a world that encourages defeat; a dark world in which evil often seems to prevail. Greed and dishonesty tend to propel people forward much more easily than goodwill and honor. Cheating and lying often seem to lead down the road to success in our culture. Love and respect are often scorned and considered outdated and old-fashioned.

How did that last paragraph make you feel? Heavy? Dark? Pea green? Like a dark, thick forest was engulfing you?

Stop! Think fresh green grass, Granny Smith apples, and wide open spaces. That's God's plan for our lives, our eternity and our impact. We are not meant to feel at home in this sinful, dark world. This is a temporary dwelling place for those of us who are followers of Christ. We are meant to be the brightening agents and the lights of the world.

So let's get coloring! It's time to water that dry grass and shine the light on those dark forests. Our world desperately needs it, and so do you and I.

"You are the light of the world. A city on a hill cannot be hidden." Matthew 5:14 (NIV)

CHAPTER 2—WHAT DOES
IT LOOK LIKE?

What does it look like to be a bright spot in this dark world? What does that even mean? It means we are supposed to be different, to stand out, to make others take a second look. We aren't meant to blend in and be like everyone else, although that is exactly what the world calls us to do.

It's uncomfortable to be different. It's frowned upon to make waves and cause people to think twice before they act. It makes others antsy, and it definitely isn't encouraged.

We live in a world that encourages us to go along to get along. We are told to accept the status quo and keep our mouths shut about others' lifestyles and morals and to mind our own business. More and more, we are expected to keep our beliefs regarding right and wrong, moral and immoral, to ourselves. We are told that we should keep this part of ourselves private, separate from everything else we do.

This attitude is permeating our society and affecting our children at a younger and younger age. Schools are denying children the right to pray in public. Some have even gone so far as refusing to pledge allegiance to the flag because of the phrase "Under God" and trying to remove "In God We Trust" from our money. The world and its king, Satan, are trying desperately to hide God and all that He stands for.

In Sunday school, I learned the song, "This Little Light of Mine," which states, "Hide it under a bushel. No! I'm going to let it shine." The world is trying desperately to hide God's light under a bushel, but God says, "No!" We are to shine. We are to be the light that shows people which way will lead to hope and freedom, which way is truth and love and will lead to eternity in Christ.

This is not a safe, easy, or smooth path. It goes against the grain of the world. It's difficult, and it's exactly what we are called to do and be.

So, again I ask, what does this look like? First, let me tell you what it does not look like. It is not the man standing on the street corner warning the passerby that he is doomed and going to eternal damnation. It is not the well-dressed Bible-study attending small group of women who gossip together and snicker behind the backs of those whom they do not believe are living a pure enough life. It is not even the popular youth group teens who will only associate with other youth group kids and steer clear of those who don't come from the right homes.

No. Jesus walked amongst sinners. He ate with them and loved them, and He treated each of them with respect and mercy.

Shouldn't we do the same? We are to live in this world but not be of the world. John 17:14-16 (NIV) says, "I have given them your word, and the world has hated them, for they are not of the world any more than I am from the world. My prayer is not that you take them out of the world but that you protect them from the evil one. They are not of the world even as I am not of it."

God intends us to walk amongst those who are lost. He does not call us to follow them or to walk amongst them and act as if we, too, are lost. No, we are to be the light walking along the narrow path of honesty, respect, honor, humility, love, and forgiveness. Others should sense that we are different and that we have a light about us that draws them to us. It is by example, not force, that we are to lead others to Christ.

Have you ever met a person who lives this kind of life? Have you met a light, one who sees the world through gratitude-colored glasses and makes everyone around them feel more at peace? I have. It is rare, but it is possible.

Her name is Laura, and she is the wife of one of the pastors at our church. She is quiet, gentle and kind, and she emanates such peace when I'm around her. I can sense her love for God and for her husband, as well as a love for all those around her.

She is not forceful in her faith, but every time I am around her, I want to be more like her—more in love with God, more respectful of my husband, and gentler in my words and ways. I don't want to be like her in an envious sort of way. I respect her and look up to her. She encourages me through her actions and demeanor, not just her words, to be more like Christ.

I believe God puts people in our lives to encourage us and to spur us on to all He wants for us. He puts others in our path to be examples to us. I want to continue to learn and grow into a woman God can use in someone else's life like he is using Laura in mine. I would love to be that inspiration to someone, that example of who they want to be in Christ.

God may never give me the satisfaction of ever knowing if I am that person to someone, but He may. My job is to strive to be that light to someone else, let God use me and trust that He is. I don't have to reach a certain 'holiness' or perfection before I can be used by God. He can use me right where I am today.

God has a plan for each of us, and we need to know and believe that He is working that plan out in our life right now. We may not see it clearly yet, but believe it, know it, celebrate it. God is using you. Are you willing? Do you dare make yourself available to Him? Please do. It is what you were created for, and it will fill your deepest longings for significance.

Scripture to Feast On:

"For I know the plans I have for you," declares the Lord. "Plans to prosper you and not to harm you; plans to give you and hope and a future." Jeremiah 29:11 (NIV)

To Do:

Ask God to reveal to you someone in your life you can look up to, someone who emanates Christ's character to you and to others. If you don't have such a person in your life, ask God to provide one for you.

CHAPTER 3—BE POSITIVE

We are taught from an early age to notice what is wrong with a situation, what doesn't belong, or who doesn't fit in. Think about it. I remember watching *Sesame Street* and being asked the same question over and over: Which one doesn't belong? On the screen were pictures of several items or characters, all having something in common except for one. Which one doesn't belong? What is not right with this picture?

Then, throughout childhood, adolescence and even adulthood, we are taught that different is bad. We learn to hone in on our differences and notice what is not right with ourselves or another person instead of focusing on what is right, what is similar, or what is comfortable and familiar. Every situation has some good in it. Each individual has positive attributes about him or her. Every life has received some amazing blessings.

I admit that each and every person I've met, including myself, has some unattractive qualities or things we would like to change about ourselves. We've also all known heartache, some more than others.

But what if we chose, each and every day, to focus on what is right in ourselves and in our world instead of focusing on what is wrong? What if we acknowledged the negatives but chose to focus instead on the positives?

Our world would be a much more pleasant place to be. We would be more pleasant. Those around us would sense our positive energy, and we would draw more and more positivity and blessings into our lives.

Of course, I know there is still reality. There is darkness and sin in our world. There is suffering and heartache, and, yes, we need to acknowledge these things and deal with them. Then we need to give them up to God our Father and try our hardest to not focus on them.

I'm not suggesting we can never be downtrodden or that it's not important to grieve at times. God acknowledges in His Word that there is a time and a season for each of these things. Ecclesiastes 3 (NIV) says, "There is a time for everything, a season for every activity under the heavens.... A time to weep and a time to laugh ... a time to mourn and a time to dance ... a time to tear and a time to mend ... a time to be silent and a time to speak ... a time for war and a time for peace."

Even Jesus mourned. He hurt. He cried many times throughout His story.

But then God tells us to focus on the positive. He instructs us in Philippians 4:8 (NIV) that, "Whatever is true, whatever is noble, whatever is right, whatever is pure, whatever is lovely, whatever is excellent or praiseworthy, think about such things."

God is telling us to look at the positive, not the negative. How refreshing! God believes in positive thinking!

God commands us to do this, and He will give us the strength and ability to do so. Ask Him for help. He wants this for you.

Why is this important? Why can't we just go on, continuing to feel sorry for ourselves, wallowing in self-pity and eliciting pity and support from others? Wouldn't it be easier to just continue to do what we've always done? Possibly, but it's not God's will for His children.

Remember, we are to be the light of the world. We cannot be negative and pessimistic and still attract others to Christ.

But we are not just called to do this for others' benefit. It will light up our own lives as well, and God wants this for us. He wants to bless you, and he wants you to bless those around you. I fully believe in the power of positive thinking and positive speaking. It can change your world in no time.

This can only be done by changing your attitude, focusing on the positive and drawing more and more of God's light into the realm of your life.

This will change your reality. It will change your outlook, and it will change you.

Scripture to Feast On:

"And I am certain that God, who began the good work within you, will carry it on to completion until the day of Christ Jesus." Philippians 1:6 (GWT)

To Do:

For the next week, first thing in the morning or last thing before bed, list three things you are grateful for. Thank God for these things and try to think on them as often as you can throughout the day.

CHAPTER 4—PLAN A

I have a plaque hanging next to my bathroom mirror that says, "Live to Make God Famous." Every day, as I'm getting ready and making my outside self presentable to the world, I read it. It reminds me that even more important than putting on my makeup, straightening my hair or choosing a cute outfit is preparing my inner self for the day ahead and for the souls I will come in contact with.

It's usually subconscious, but I often make a decision right then and there if I'm going to focus on that today or not. I hate to admit it, but some days I just have too much to think about or am way too busy to bother with such a focus. Those are exactly the kinds of days when I need it most.

If I'm not on guard, Satan will have a heyday with my busy, "so-important," sidetracked, crazy schedule. He is lying in wait for just such moments when we are not dressed in the armor of God and, therefore, are vulnerable. We are reminded in Ephesians 6 to put on the belt of truth, the breastplate of righteousness, the shield of faith, and the helmet of salvation.

It's a decision we need to make daily, sometimes hourly, in order to keep ourselves on track. It's God's purpose for us. He calls us to it. He expects it of us. We are the hands and feet of Christ, and we are His Plan A for this world. He has no Plan B.

What does this mean? It means that people are either going to see Christ through us or they are not going to see Christ at all.

Does this overwhelm you? It overwhelms me until I remember that "I can do all things through Christ who strengthens me," according to Philippians 4:13 (KJV). That is a promise from God Himself. He never calls us to do something impossible. When He calls us to something, He makes a way, and He is calling us to glorify Him. He wants us to reflect His light onto this dark and lost world.

How? Step by step. One day at a time, one moral decision at a time, and one positive, loving word at a time.

We can do this, you and I, because God is on our side, showing us the way and giving us the wisdom and the tools to make Him famous in a world that desperately longs for a Hero. It's important to remember that you might be the only "Jesus" they see.

Have you ever heard of the Great Commission? It is God's call to His Church (that's us!) to go out into all the nations making disciples. He wasn't just talking to his twelve disciples or even just to the Church of Christ's time on earth. They are no longer here to spread God's Word. They long ago passed the torch to us, and now we are the ones who are to go out into all the nations spreading God's Good News.

Some of us are actually called to go to far off countries bringing Christ to those who have never heard of Him. God will bless those people and enable them in their service to Him.

But many of us will never hear that call to mission work. It's not God's will that every one of us travels to the far ends of the earth to share His Word. However, that doesn't let the rest of us off the hook. Oh, no! He commands and expects the rest of us to be His disciples right where we are. Bloom where you're planted. In other words, be the light to your spouse, your children, your neighbors. Don't forget that God also placed your banker, your grocer, your cab driver, and your son's teacher in your midst as well. These are the people He wants you to reach.

Does that mean you have to preach to the bank teller as she is counting out your money? Of course not. But what it does mean is that you are to be kind, be trustworthy, be positive. Smile and show them that something's different about you. Draw them to what you have. Christ will do the rest.

"Bloom Where You are Planted."

Afghan Proverb (Also see 1 Corinthians 7:7-24)

Scripture to Feast On:

"Let your light shine before men in such a way that they may see your good works, and glorify your Father who is in Heaven." Matthew 5:16 (NIV)

To Do:

Who has God placed in your life and on your heart that He wants you to be a light to? Ask Him to reveal this person(s) to you and consciously connect with them this week. God will lead you and give you the wisdom you need.

CHAPTER 5—HOW IT'S DONE

W e've talked about why we are to be the light of the world. We've talked about what it looks like and how it benefits us, others and God. But how exactly do we do it? How can we be the light when we are surrounded by darkness and have our own set of hardships, temptations, and difficulties? It sounds impossible, but it's not. Again, I go back to God's Word that tells us that with Christ all things are possible. Throughout Scripture, we are reminded that when He calls us to something, He also equips us.

Does that mean it will be easy? Does that mean we will never fail to do so? No way. One thing God never promises us is that it will be easy to follow His commands, and that includes this one.

So how do we do it? With perseverance, with determination. We choose to let God's light shine through us, and we choose it over and over and over again.

Will we fall? Yes. Should we give up? Never. In Hebrews, we are told to run with perseverance the path set out for us. (Hebrews 12:1)

What is perseverance? I looked it up online, and it said that perseverance is commitment, hard work, patience, and endurance. It is being able to bear difficulties calmly and without complaint. That's a tall order, but it's one we can fulfill with God's help.

Will it always be difficult? No. Some days it feels so natural, so much a part of who we are. We feel close to our Heavenly Father and can feel His light emanating off us. We are patient to the person in line in front of us at the grocery store who has twenty different coupons that need to be manually entered in one by one. We smile at the driver in the lane next to us who glares through his window, throwing daggers our way. We're patient with our children, our spouse, and everyone else we come in contact with. Some days are just that way—filled with joy and peace and gratitude.

But some days aren't. Those are the days that call for perseverance. Those are the days we choose to obey anyway. Those are the days we need to try again and again, over and over asking God to help us, give us strength, give us patience, and give us clarity. And He will.

He will not stop helping us become more and more like Him until the day of completion. (Philippians 1:6) Would God bother to give us that promise if we were expected to get it right the first time we tried, or the tenth, or the fiftieth?

No. God knows that we will never be perfect at following His call, but He wants us to persevere in our efforts, ask forgiveness when we fall, and then try all over again.

That's what will set us apart from others. We need to be willing to let God work in us, even when it doesn't come naturally or easily.

One of the best ways to prepare your heart and mind to be available for God's work is to connect with Him daily on an intimate level. I have noticed that when I skip my morning quiet time with the Lord, I have a lot less patience and peace to share with others. I have learned that setting aside 20 to 45 minutes of time alone with God, in His Word and in prayer, every morning is one of the most important things I can do for myself as well as for my spouse and children.

If I'm having a really difficult day, easily losing my patience with people and focusing on the negative more than I should, I can often trace it back to my morning ritual—or lack thereof. Maybe I got interrupted by my daughter who had a sewing emergency and came to me desperately needing a rush button-sewing job on her favorite sweater. Or maybe one of the cats threw up on the living room floor, and I spent my precious quiet time cleaning it up. Sometimes I just catch myself daydreaming through my half-hour quiet time instead of focusing on God and getting my heart set right for the day.

Whatever the case may be, life happens. The point is that I notice a big difference in my outlook on those days that I didn't—or I couldn't—make God a priority for a little slice in time. I miss it. I long for it. God calls me to it.

He calls us each to it, but time with Him might look very different for you from the way it does for me. Just listen to what you're called to. You'll know. Listen and follow and know that He is changing you. He is shaping you. You are becoming more and more of a light.

Scripture to Feast On:

Let us run with perseverance the race marked out for us. Hebrews 12:1 (NIV)

To Do:

Make a list of some common excuses you have for not persevering, rather it be in studying God's word, exercising, healthy eating, keeping in contact with friends, etc. Try to be aware this week of when one of these excuses pops up. Counter it with Hebrews 12:1.

CHAPTER 6—HOLD TIGHT

What about when it's difficult, or maybe even seems impossible, to see any light whatsoever, let alone *be* a light? Sometimes all we can see or feel is darkness. Grief. Despair. Heartbreak. There is no hope to hold on to. There is no light at the end of the tunnel, only more darkness. What can we do then?

Hold on. Wait. Cling. It's okay to be completely dependent on God to do all the work during these dark times. Sometimes it's all we can do to get up in the morning and trudge through another day.

Our Father knows when we have NOTHING left to offer Him or others. He understands this. He accepts us in that place.

There is a time for everything under the sun (Eccl. 3). There is a time to give and a time to share and a time to shine. But there is also a time to take and need and depend.

Four years ago, I went through an incredibly dark time in my life. There was a period of months when I felt as if I had lost almost everything that was important to me.

I lost contact with my family for over five months, while at the same time losing my fiancé-to-be over issues of infidelity and lies. Because of these things, I lost my confidence in my abilities as a mother to protect my children from people who bring harm and pain into their lives.

Two months into this painful time, my best friend, Sara, whom I felt was my lifeline at the time, informed me she was moving to Haiti to be a long-term missionary. It was a devastating blow to an already fragile hold on sanity that I felt.

She and I first met while on a mission trip together in Haiti several years prior. While I was so proud of her and supportive of her following God's lead in her life, I felt like the floor had opened up and swallowed me whole with that final blow.

I remember trying to be strong for the kids, going through the motions of what was expected of me. But once the kids were tucked into bed, I would curl up in a fetal position on the floor of my living room in front of the fireplace and weep.

I cried until it hurt. I cried until I couldn't cry anymore. I did this night after night after night.

I couldn't call my family. They were still angry at me for letting this man into the children's and my life. I couldn't call my ex-fiancé. He had proven to be everything my family said he was and exactly what he had promised me he wasn't. I couldn't call Sara (although I often ended up calling her anyway), because I didn't want her to feel guilty for leaving me during this time. And I definitely wasn't going to talk to my children about how much pain I was in, although I'm sure they were well aware.

I would just cry. I often didn't even talk to God during this time. All I could do was picture Him holding me while I lay on the floor. I just held on. I waited.

And He was there. Just there with me. I felt it. I knew it. At one point, I remembered the saying, "You don't know that God is all you need until He is all you have." It was true. I had Him, and He would never leave me nor forsake me. He had promised.

This went on for weeks. Every day I cried, some more than others. Until one day when Sara asked me how I was doing, I was finally able to say," Well, I didn't cry today." Soon it became two or three days, and then I finally was able to go a whole week without crying.

I was healing! My grief was subsiding. How? I waited. I held on. That's all I knew how to do or could do. God did the rest. He took me through it. It was painful, and it felt oh-so-long. But God was there with me the entire time.

I look back now at that dark time and realize that I will never be the same. We never are the same after a truly painful experience. We aren't supposed to be. God uses it to grow us and strengthen us.

Would I want to go through something like that again in order to grow and mature? No way! I would never have signed up for that if I knew what was in store for me and the kids. But I can say I'm thankful for it now. I can say I came out stronger because of it.

It was an incredibly long, dark winter, but now we are living in the beautiful springtime that came after.

I am happily married to the most wonderful, God-honoring man who loves me and loves my children more than I could have ever dreamed. My relationships with my family are mended and wonderfully supportive, and my children are thriving and growing into beautiful, godly people.

I am so grateful and so blessed, and all I did was hold on and wait. Sometimes that's all we can do. But God comes through for us every time.

Are we called to shine God's light for others in this dark world? Yes. And God expects this of us. But He also knows our limitations. He is well aware of our struggles, and He will do the work when we can't. He tells us, "I will never leave you nor forsake you," Hebrews 13:5 (ESV).

Scripture to Feast On:

"God is our refuge and strength, an ever-present help in trouble," Psalms 46:1 (NIV).

To Do:

Was there a time when you felt completely alone? Did you recognize God's presence? In what ways did He make Himself known to you?

INGREDIENTS FOR GROWTH

We all know that in order to have lush, green grass or flourishing gardens, several ingredients are needed: sunshine, water, good soil, and possibly even some good fertilizer.

It's no different for us. We need certain things in order to continue to shine God's light in this world: focus, determination, and quiet time with our Father.

That is what the second half of this book is for. I want to get you started on the path to a lifelong journey of gratefulness and light.

It is said that new habits form if we do something consistently for thirty days. My challenge to you is to make time with God a priority for the next thirty days and see what He does with it.

This section is designed to be read one day at a time. Set aside 20 minutes a day to focus on the daily entry. Let God speak to you. Spend some time with Him in prayer and reflection. He will use this time to get your mind set on things above.

Use the scripture in each day's passage as a starting point. Get your Bible out and read the entire chapter in which the verse is found.

I notice a difference on the days I begin by spending time with God. Try this for the next thirty days and see if you discern a difference as well.

God's Word encourages us to regularly spend time with Him:

Your Word is a lamp unto my feet and a light unto my path. Psalms 119:105 (KJV)

Like newborn infants, long for the pure spiritual milk, that by it you may grow up into salvation. 1 Peter 2:2 (ESV)

All scripture is breathed out by God and profitable for teaching, for reproof, for correction and for training in righteousness, that the man of God may be complete, equipped for every good work. 2 Timothy 3:16-17 (ESV)

DAY 1—ARISE AND SHINE!

"Get out of bed, Jerusalem! Wake up. Put your face in the sunlight.
God's bright glory has risen for you. The whole earth is wrapped in
darkness, all people sunk in deep darkness. But God rises on you; His
sunrise glory breaks over you. Nations will come to your light, kings to
your sunburst brightness. Look up! Look around!"
Isaiah 60:1-4 (MSG)

I f this isn't a call to action, I don't know what is! God is calling you. You are needed! Remember, you are His plan A.

Start today knowing you have God's light inside you. You will likely encounter several, if not many, people who do not know this light. Show it to them. Smile. Offer a helping hand without expecting anything in return. Be patient and kind even when the store clerk is not. It's so easy for us to match peoples' moods when we interact with them. For example, if the woman in line in front of us is abrupt and snappy, we often respond back in kind. Instead, assume she is having a really hard day and that's why she's frowning. Would that cause you to treat her differently? Make it your goal to try to make her smile before you part ways. What a fun challenge!

These small actions take so little of us, and yet they very well may make the difference in the life of someone else. Make a conscious effort today to shine a ray of God's love on someone who needs it. Everyone needs it at times. Choose someone (or several people) and do it. Ask God to open your eyes and "nudge" you when it's needed, and see what He does.

Reflection:

Who did you shine God's light on today? Why did you choose them? How did it feel to you? Did you notice a difference in their demeanor or attitude? What about your own?

DAY 2—REAL LIFE

Ask yourself, "Am I really living, or am I just existing?"

"For I know the plans I have for you," declares the Lord,

"plans to prosper you and not to harm you;

plans to give you a hope and a future."

Jeremiah 29:11 (NIV)

I quote this verse often, usually to remind myself or others that God has it all figured out even if we don't. However, there is another praise in this scripture. God is not just telling us that He has our problems figured out for us. He's also telling us that His plans are to prosper us and to give us hope.

That doesn't sound like God's plans are for us to just survive or exist. No! He wants us to excel! He has great big plans for your life.

At times I struggle with living my life on autopilot. I am so busy, stressed, worried or all of the above, and I go into 'survival mode.' I just put one foot in front of the other, crossing tasks off my to-do list and waiting until I can drop back into bed at the end of the day. We all get this way at times, and at times it's even necessary. However, don't get stuck in this rut. It should be temporary and short-lived. Pay attention to if you are truly living or are just surviving.

Don't settle for ho-hum. Don't let Satan convince you that survival mode is as good as it gets. God wants to PROSPER you!

Reflection:

What does "prosper" mean to you? What do you think it means to God? How do you imagine these two definitions can manifest themselves in your life?

DAY 3—LITTLE JOYS

Often, our joy comes not from big, exciting events that happen to us but from the little, daily jewels God places in our lives. When I find myself feeling down in the dumps or bored, I often just pick up a pen and paper and jot down five to ten things I am grateful for. These are, more often than not, the small joys I can sometimes take for granted.

I love holding a purring cat in my lap. I love and appreciate how my two dogs are always happy to see me. I am grateful that my husband faithfully leaves me a sweet note on the counter next to my coffee mug before he leaves for work. I appreciate that my fourteen-year-old son still likes to hang out and watch TV with me occasionally. I am so grateful that my sixteen-year-old daughter shares her fears, uncertainties, and sorrows with me. There are times when I just sit and listen to the rain outside my window and appreciate my warm, cozy home and a nice hot cup of coffee.

Do you realize that God gave us all these little treats? He didn't have to give us laughter and snuggling and fuzzy pets. He did it to please us. He did it to add joy to our daily lives. How great is that?

"This is the day that the Lord has made;
let us rejoice and be glad in it."
Psalms 118:24 (ESV)

Reflection:

What are five things you are grateful for today? Try to remember these and thank God for them as they pop into your mind or as they bless your day.

Get a nice journal or notebook, and start your own Gratitude Journal. Write in it daily or when you need a reminder of all you have to be thankful for.

DAY 4—STRETCH

I love to stretch. There's something about it that just makes me feel alive. It hurts and feels good all at the same time. Several times a day I stop what I'm doing and just stretch. (This is usually done in private, but those I'm comfortable around are used to seeing me do this and no longer find it strange—or maybe they just stopped mentioning it.)

God wants you to stretch. Emotionally stretch; spiritually stretch; personally stretch. God doesn't want you to stay stagnant—never growing, never moving. He wants you to step out of your comfort zone. Climb out of the pit you've settled into. It might hurt, but it will feel so good too!

There have been times God has stretched me when I didn't think I wanted to be stretched. One such time was when I was asked to give my testimony to a group of Christians I considered much more mature than me in their walk. It was so scary, and I really didn't feel qualified, but God made it clear that He wanted me to do it. I went out of my comfort zone and obeyed Him, and that experience helped me become a stronger, more confident version of myself.

There are also times when I have chosen to stretch myself. Writing this book is one example. I've never written a book before, and it's scary. What if nobody thinks it's good? What if no one reads it? What if people judge me or think less of me when I share my weaknesses and hardships? These are all fears that have run through my mind, but I chose instead to ignore them. I chose to go out of my comfort zone and stretch myself. Sometimes it's not comfortable. Sometimes it hurts, but it's also exciting and exhilarating, and life-enhancing—just like physically stretching.

Sometimes we are stretched by changing circumstances we have no control over. But, sometimes we need to make those changes ourselves.

"Brethren, I don't regard myself as yet having taken hold,
but one thing I do: Forgetting the things which are behind,
and stretching forward to the things which are before."
Philippians 3:13 (WEB)
God wants you to stretch.

Reflection:

In what ways is God calling you to stretch? Are there ways you've wanted to stretch yourself but haven't? Ask God to show you where you've grown stagnant and need to step out of your comfort zone.

DAY 5—SIGNS

As I was reading my devotional this morning, I read this verse:
"Give me a sign of your goodness, that my enemies may see it and be put to shame. For you, O LORD, have helped me and comforted me."
Psalms 86:17 (NIV)

My study went on to encourage me to go ahead and ask God for a sign that He's there for me. I quickly said a silent prayer, telling God I thought it would be pretty cool if he gave me some sort of sign—just for fun.

Then I forgot about it and went on with my day. And what a busy, stressful day it was! I had way more work to do than I normally do and proceeded to get very stressed out and very, very grumpy. Luckily, nobody was home to bear my wrath, but God was there.

And guess what—I said a few things under my breath that weren't very righteous. I immediately proceeded to apologize to God and ask His forgiveness. (I tend to have to do this quite often.) I didn't even have a very good attitude while I was apologizing!

Anyway, I gave myself a break, sitting outside on the back patio. I closed my eyes and forced myself to take some deep breaths and just relax.

After a couple minutes, I opened my eyes and guess what I saw painted across the bright blue sky? Two jet airplane trails. Now, this may not sound very amazing to you, but the greatest part was what shape the two vapor trails formed. A perfect cross! Huge, bright, and so clearly meant for me!

It was like God was winking at me, playing with me and, to be honest with you, showing off a bit. I loved it! It put a smile on my face and a skip in my step. I was able to get back to my work with a much better attitude, all because God showed up.

Reflection:

Have you ever asked God to give you a sign of His presence? Ask Him to, but leave it up to Him how and when. It's really fun waiting to see what He'll pull off next. Give it a try!

DAY 6—PRAYING FOR YOU

How many times have you told someone you would pray for them or their loved one? How often do you actually follow through with prayer? I hope it's often. I hope it's every time.

Unfortunately, I've found myself forgetting time and time again to follow through with consistent prayer for another person. I'm ashamed of this, and I've asked God to help me grow in this area.

So, now I pray every morning for my husband, my daughter, and my son—in the order they got up that day. I often choose a topic or a theme for each one for a week or two, focusing on an area in their lives I want to cover in prayer.

I have also asked God to make me blatantly aware of and responsible for the times I tell coworkers, friends, or others that I will pray for their situation.

We are called to carry each other in prayer. I don't want to take this lightly, and I definitely would like others to remember me in prayer when it's needed.

Therefore, confess your sins to one another and pray for one another, that you may be healed. The prayer of the righteous person has great power as it is working.
James 5:16 (ESV)

Reflection:

Ask God to make you acutely aware of those times you utter the words, "I'll be praying for you." Take it seriously, and take it to God in prayer. The Lord will help you grow in this area, because it is His will.

DAY 7—RENT OR OWN?

O nce you have accepted Jesus Christ as your personal Savior, you are a child of God! You share in the same inheritance as Jesus himself! Do you live your life this way? Do you own your part in God's story, or do you act more like a renter in God's church?

We all treat things differently when we own them as opposed to when we rent them. Think about how you've treated the cars you've rented. Sure, you are responsible and probably abide by all the rules laid out in the contract you signed. But would you go above and beyond what's required of you? Would you spend your own time and money washing, waxing, and vacuuming the rental car if it's not required of you? I doubt it. I wouldn't.

What about a house or an apartment you've rented? Would you use your own hard-earned money to put on a new roof or landscape the property? Probably not.

God wants us to act like owners of His kingdom. He doesn't want us to act like renters and just fulfill the minimum requirements. He wants us to put our heart and soul into our service to Him. He wants us to OWN the mission of reaching the lost and looking after orphans and widows.

For we are God's fellow workers.
You are God's field, God's building.
1 Corinthians 3:9 (ESV)

Reflection:

Ask God to show you ways you are acting more like a renter than an owner in His mission. In what ways is God nudging you to take more pride of ownership in your church, in your walk, in His story?

DAY 8—STAND FIRM

"Be on your guard; stand firm in the faith;
be men of courage; be strong."
I Corinthians 16: 13 (NIV)

I really needed this verse last night. As a matter of fact, I need it often. Yesterday was a difficult day for me, and I was at a loss for why until this morning.

Satan was having a heyday at my expense last night. I let my guard down, and he pounced on the opportunity.

I hate to admit it, but I had gone several days—almost an entire week—without spending any true quiet time with the Lord. My son had just started his summer vacation, and I decided to treat myself to sleeping in as well.

Now, this isn't wrong in itself. What made it a problem is that I didn't schedule my regular early morning devotional/prayer time for another part of the day. Instead, I just dropped it. Boy, it sure didn't take long for Satan to jump in and start filling my head with lies.

I left myself vulnerable to his tactics because I wasn't filling my heart and mind with God's truths.

I started listening to the father of lies as he told me that God hasn't blessed me enough financially, in my marriage, in my career—all of which are false. I began to feel resentment toward my husband, in a way also blaming him for all my unhappiness. Satan loves to erode away marriages, especially Christ-centered ones.

I couldn't shake the overwhelming feelings of resentment, disappointment, and hopelessness last night, so I just went to bed without bothering to say anything to my husband or kids. God woke me up with a very clear directive to get up and get in His Word. I did, and that's when my eyes were opened to the fact that Satan was in full-blown attack mode and I better put on my full armor.

I spent the rest of the morning reminding myself and thanking God for all the big and small blessings He's showered me with. God is always with us, and He is waiting for our focus to shift to and stay on Him. But never ever underestimate Satan's watchful eye. When you let your guard down, he will swoop in and do as much damage as possible before you realize it and you call on your Savior.

Stand firm. Be on guard. Never forget how important your focus is.

"By standing firm, you will gain life."
Luke 21:19 (NIV)

Reflection:

Can you relate to my story? Do you ever find yourself feeling depressed or oppressed for no good reason? What do you find yourself focusing on during these times? Try to switch your focus to thoughts of gratitude and God's blessings.

DAY 9—BE STILL

Be still and know that I am God.
Psalms 46:10 (NIV)

What does it mean to be still? How does that look? It's almost a foreign concept to most of us. I know it is to me. We are often running around from place to place, dropping off kids, picking up groceries, running from one expectation of ourselves to another.

Is that wrong? No. Life is busy. God understands that. He is not calling us to check out of reality, only to take a break now and then. In fact, He tells us to take a break once a week in the form of a Sabbath day. Sometimes I think of Sunday as just another day to get the house cleaned up or run some errands. I need to be reminded that the Sabbath is meant to be a day to slow down and focus on my Father.

I also believe it's important to take minibreaks often throughout our busy day. Why is this so important? It's important because God doesn't want to have to fight for our attention. He knows how busy our days are and also how our minds can run nonstop. He calls us to consciously shut out the clamoring of the world and focus on Him.

He is always there with us, but it's imperative that we stop and listen. He has a lot to say to us, and He isn't going to shout to get our attention. We must be prepared and ready to hear His still, small voice.

This is a choice. We must consciously choose to be still before our Lord.

Reflection:

Take time to sit quietly, be still, and hear from God. Shhhh … wait for Him to speak. Do you make a habit of this, or does it feel awkward and unnatural to you? Choose to make being still a regular part of your busy life.

DAY 10—SMILE

We spend a lot of time trying to find happiness. We read books on finding our purpose, becoming successful, and finding prosperity in life. Have you ever noticed how popular the 'Self-Help' section is at Barnes and Noble? I have spent a lot of time and money on these types of books myself. None of these goals and aspirations are wrong, but God does not want them to be our primary focus.

Our ultimate goal in life should be to please God; to make Him smile down on us. He created us for a purpose. As we read His Word, He will make it abundantly clear to us what He wants us to do.

Numbers 6:25 (NLT) says, "May the Lord smile on you and be gracious to you." Choose to live every day with your ultimate goal being to bring a smile to the Creator's face. What a fun target to aim for.

Break out in a worship song while you are doing the dinner dishes. Say a kind word to the stranger next to you on the bus. Offer to let the lady with only a couple purchases go ahead of you in the grocery line. Give your spouse a big thank you hug when he or she comes home from work. These are just a few fun ideas to bring God's smile down on you.

Reflection:

What are one or two things you can do today to bring a smile to God's face? Try to keep this goal in mind, whether at work, home, or anywhere else and see how it improves your demeanor.

DAY 11—BALANCE

I n order to function at our best, we all need balance in our lives. When I find myself getting more easily irritated with my husband or children, I know to check my balance. If I am feeling depressed or hopeless, I evaluate the balance in my days. Sometimes I find myself less able to withstand temptation to sin, and I know that I need to stop and check in with myself.

I have learned that I get out of balance when the withdrawals from my energy tank are greater than the deposits. I like to think of my life balance like a bank balance. If I keep allowing things or people to suck the energy out of my account without making plenty of deposits, I am very quickly depleted. When I get to that point, I am irritable, grumpy, sad, hopeless, lack energy, lack love, and definitely lack patience.

One thing I found very helpful was to make a list of things that drain me and a list of things that fill me up. These things will be different for each of us.

For example, I am easily drained by too much noise. I call it "noise clutter." Hearing the TV constantly in the background drains me. I'm the same way if my house is messy or cluttered. I feel irritable and snappy after a while. Some people thrive with background noise and can't focus without it.

Other things that drain me are sitting at the computer, talking on the phone, and whiny kids. There are many other things on my list, and they are all personal to me. It's my responsibility to know what they are and how to limit them in my day-to-day life.

Of course, we can't eliminate all energy drains from our life no matter how much we wish we could. Therefore, it's also important to have a list of things that add to our energy stores. For me, it was easy to come up with that list, and most of them are free and simple to accomplish.

For example, a nice walk by myself does wonders for my attitude. A hot bubble bath, snuggling with my cats, feeling sunshine on my face, spending quiet time with God and a nice, hot cup of coffee are all energy deposits for me. Of course, I also love going on vacation, buying a cute new outfit and going out to a nice dinner, but these tend to happen less frequently.

Try to find a good balance every day, and notice how much more patient and loving you are with those around you.

And he said unto them, "Come ye yourselves apart into a desert place, and rest awhile: for there were many coming and going, and they had no leisure so much as to eat."
Mark 6:31 (KJV)

Reflection:

Make a list of at least ten things that drain your energy bank. Try to limit your exposure to these things. Next, make a list of ten (or more) things that add pep to your step and give you energy. Add as many of these as possible every day!

DAY 12—TRUST

Trust in the Lord with all your heart,

and lean not on your own understanding.

Proverbs 3:5 (KJV)

I 've known this verse most of my life and have often recited it to myself in times of uncertainty and fear. But I have just recently realized that it's much easier to depend on God and His promises when I'm under extreme stress and am at a loss as to how to move forward in an area of my life. I am not as inclined to lean on Him or even ask Him for guidance for the smaller, daily stressors.

I tend to rely on my own wisdom and guidance during those times, forgetting that God wants to guide me at all times.

Our Father doesn't want us to call on Him only when we have tried everything else first. He is not supposed to be just a last resort when all else fails.

God wants us to trust in Him and rely on Him all the time. When I am having a heart-to-heart with my teenager, I can (and should) call on Christ to give me wisdom with my words. He wants me to call on Him when I need patience with my spouse or wisdom when I am not sure if I should make a particular purchase.

God knows how limited our knowledge is. He has made Himself available to us as a Life-Guide, in big and in small matters. Don't put Him in a box and only open it when you've exhausted all other options and tried what you know first. Go to Him first and see how confident and supported you feel in all matters.

Reflection:

Proverbs 3:5-6 continues, *"In all your ways acknowledge Him, and He shall direct your paths."*

What would this look like in your life? Memorize these verses and quote them throughout the day. Try to remember to ask God for direction and wisdom from the beginning.

DAY 13—LOVE

These three things remain: Faith, Hope and Love.

But the greatest of these is Love.

I Corinthians 13:13 (NIV)

Love is patient, love is kind. It does not envy, it does not boast, it is not

proud. It is not rude, it is not self-seeking, it is not easily angered,

it keeps no record of wrongs. Love does not delight in evil but rejoices

with the truth. It always protects, always trusts, always hopes,

always perseveres. Love never fails.

I Corinthians 13:4-8a (NIV).

I have heard these verses quoted many times over the course of my life. Love is mentioned over 500 times in the Bible, yet it's never really been a focus of mine. Of course, love is important. Of course, I want love in my life. I love my husband, my kids, my sisters and their children and spouses. I love my parents and my closest friends. I love God.

Recently, however, God has been convicting me to *really* love others. He has been calling me to walk in love.

I don't know exactly what this looks like but, as usual, God is convicting me of what it does not look like.

When I start to gossip about someone, I hear God say, "Love," and it stops me in my tracks. When I am beginning to get impatient with someone, I hear Him say, "Love." And when I find myself judging others because they are doing life differently from the way I do it or think they should be, God gently whispers, "Love."

Wow. God is growing me in several different areas I've struggled with by His simple command to "love others." It is transforming my life. I want to live differently. I want to emanate love to others, even to people who aren't my favorite.

I have no doubt this is something I will always have to lean on God for, but my goal is to become more and more like Jesus as I learn to walk in love.

Reflection:

Meditate on what it means to really walk in love. Ask God to convict you each and every time you fail to do so. If you want an idea of what walking in love looks like, read more about the way Jesus lived His life. (Read Matthew 11:29, John 13:13-16, 1 Corinthians 11:1, Ephesians 5:1-2, Colossians 3:13).

DAY 14—PARADIGM SHIFT

I t's been three months since I've written. I love writing. It's my passion. But a good, solid three months have passed between writing day thirteen and writing day fourteen. I wanted to write, but I had what some people call "writer's block." I call it "gratitude block."

I wanted to feel grateful. I'm writing a book called "Gratitude Greens," for goodness sake! But I've been struggling. Over the past several months, I have felt more frustrated and even just plain ticked off rather than sunny and grateful. I felt let down.

Over the past year, my husband and I have worked very consistently on reaching several financial goals we felt God had put on our hearts. We paid off several bills, saved some money to go on a summer family vacation, and even saved up enough cash to buy my husband a little run-around truck to get to and from work so our sixteen-year-old daughter could drive one of the more reliable cars we have.

We felt pretty proud of ourselves for meeting each of the goals as we were able to cross them off our list. I think that's where we went wrong. We were proud of ourselves and forgot to praise our Heavenly Father each time He enabled us to reach a goal.

All of a sudden, things began to go wrong. These weren't huge, catastrophic things, just small annoyances and frustrations. First of all, the "reliable" car we provided for our daughter completely conked out one day. We were down to sharing two cars between the three of us again, which was really tough because both kids are in sports and go to different schools, and my husband and I both work.

This was another negative undercurrent going on. The full time job I had just started was not nearly as fulfilling and Christ-centered as I had expected. There was stress and discord in the workplace, and I was expected to work extra hours during my precious family time. We had pets getting injured and incurring hundreds of dollars in vet bills. We had sprained ankles, hurt knees, mammograms, physical ailments, etc.—all costing us money left and right.

We were in the process of selling the condo I owned before we were married, and we were told that because of the poor housing market, it would cost us hundreds, if not thousands, of dollars to "get out of it."

We were so frustrated and felt like God was letting us down. We felt like we deserved a break because we had "done everything right" by working so hard to financially meet all of our goals. We even ranted and raved at God a bit.

But one thing I never stopped doing is spending time with the Lord every day. Even when I felt disillusioned, angry, and let down by Him, I still went to Him each day. I told Him how I felt. I told Him I thought He should give me a break. I told Him I wanted things to go my way for a while.

And He seemed to be silent. Where was He? Did He abandon me? What's His problem? Sometimes I even got a bit disrespectful about it.

And He waited. Until one day it dawned on me. He was providing all our needs. We weren't getting ahead financially like we wanted to, but God was providing all our needs. One by one, we were able to take care of our costs. We didn't have much left over after each paycheck, but we were always able to pay our bills. God provided our needs—not our wants, but our needs.

This was like a giant light bulb going on for me! God's always got our backs even when we wish He would bless us in different, more fun and exciting ways. He never leaves us. He never forsakes us. Even when we feel like life is letting us down at every turn, God is there, catching us when we fall.

We didn't have anything huge or horrible happen over these past few months: no deaths in the family or devastating health news. Sometimes all we can do during these horrible, dark times is lean on our Father. But it's the times in which the small disappointments and setbacks seem never-ending that it's harder to remember that He's there for those, too.

Don't forget, God wants to carry even the smaller, mere energy-draining burdens as well as the huge, impossible ones. He's here for the gray days, too, not just the pitch-black ones.

Cling to Him on the horrible days but also on the ho-hum days. He's there for you on both. It's up to you to recognize Him.

And this same God who takes care of me will supply all your needs from His glorious riches, which have been given to us in Christ Jesus.
Philippians 4:19 (NLT)

Reflection:

Can you relate to my ho-hum, nitty-gritty, constant-setbacks kind of day? If so, do you tend to forget God's got your back then, too? Focus your heart and mind on Him when you feel overwhelmed by the daily-ness of life.

Review Romans 8:28 (ESV): which says, "And we know that for those who love God all things work together for good, for those who are called according to His purpose."

DAY 15—MARGIN

Margins are the extra spaces left on the pages of books on either side of the text. I often write notes or put stars in the margins next to passages I especially like or that are especially meaningful to me. Usually, this is done in my Bible or in a significant, heartfelt book. We all need margin in our lives as well.

Creating margin in our lives is a lot like creating extra spaces around the text of the busyness of our lives. If we don't get intentional about margins, we risk filling our lives too chock-full of errands, classes, Bible studies, church, to-do lists, etc.

These are all good things, many of which need to be done. However, we need to build extra space into our mornings to spend time with our Lord without having a strict agenda. We need to leave room in our day to help a stranger with her groceries or stop to talk to a friend we run into at the store. We need to create pockets of time in which we can listen to our son's recess stories or talk to our daughter about a particular struggle she is having with friends.

There will always be those unexpected needs or conversations that pop up in our lives, just like there are always unexpected expenses coming at us from all directions.

Don't just rush from one thing on your to-do list to the next. Plan for those unforeseen events, just like you plan for miscellaneous expenses in your budget. It might be God or it might be another person you need to take time for, but create margin in your life so you are ready.

Come now, you who say, "Today or tomorrow we will go into such and such a town and spend a year there and trade and make a profit"-yet you do not know what tomorrow will bring. What is your life? For you are a mist that appears for a little time and then vanishes. Instead you ought to say, "If the Lord wills, we will live and do this or that."

As it is, you boast in your arrogance. All such boasting is evil. So whoever knows the right thing to do and fails to do it, for him it is sin.
James 4: 13-17 (ESV)

Reflection:

Read Luke 10:38-42. Are you like Martha or like Mary? Most of us have a little of each of them in us. Ask God to show you where you can create margin in your life so you will be more available to Him and to others.

DAY 16—BE OPEN

Be silent before the Lord and wait expectantly for Him.

Psalms 37:7 (HCSB)

I don't know what God has planned for me in the near future or long term. It drives me crazy to not know what the plan is or what goals I am supposed to be working toward. It "goes against my grain."

I am a planner. I am a list maker. Generally, if something is on my to-do list or on my list of goals to accomplish, it will get done. I have always taken great pride in this. Even when I was a child, my mom claimed that once I got a "bee in my bonnet," I wouldn't let it go.

But God doesn't want me to have pride in myself. He doesn't want me to feel like I have everything planned out and under control. He wants me to look to Him for His plans. He wants me to depend on Him, not on my own strong will.

Recently, God led me to a place of complete uncertainty in the future. He gave me a sense of unrest about how I was living my life and convicted me of how much my children needed me to be available. Our kids are teenagers. I was never able to completely be a stay-at-home mom even when they were very young. It seemed an unlikely time to be drawn to be home full time, but that's exactly how I felt. My husband and I both felt clearly led for me to quit my job and come home full time. We really aren't any better off financially now than we were in the past, so I don't know why we both feel such a peace about living off just one income. But we do. God has made it abundantly clear to both of us that He wants me home and available to our family.

How did He make it clear to us? Did God speak audibly to me and tell me what I had to do? No, of course not. But He did clearly speak to me. He opened my eyes to my daughter's need to have me available to talk to her in the middle of the night. He showed me how my son blossomed when I took time to sit down and really listen to him. I believe God uses circumstances, other people and our convictions and emotions to speak to each of us. We just have to be willing to listen and pay attention. My desire to be home full time with my teenagers would not go away. It was always on my mind. The more I thought about it, the more I struggled with whether or not it was fair to expect my husband to work and provide for me and his step-kids while I got to stay home all day. It would definitely make it tight financially for our family. I thought that it was asking an awful lot of my husband, and I prayed about it often. Then one day, we were on a walk, and he brought up the fact that he wanted me to be more available to the kids. This was an answer to prayer! God showed me that He was working out all the details, even convicting my husband's heart. That was when I knew God would provide and was giving me His blessing. He was opening the door, and all I had to do was step through it.

What does He have planned? I know He wants me to be the best mom I can possibly be, and I can think of many other noble things I could fill this open time with. I can think of a lot of different goals (many of them very noble goals) to work toward during my open schedule. How long will this hiatus last? Months? Years? Forever? I have no idea. But God does, and He is setting this time aside for a reason.

No matter how much I have to wrestle with myself and my natural tendency to take control, I am determined to wait on God and remain open to His plan for the future. I will wait until He clearly and vividly points me in a certain direction instead of desperately looking for what direction I think I should be headed.

Reflection:

Are there areas of your life that you have forgotten to hand over to God? Ask Him to show you anything you are holding onto that you need to give over to Him. Ask God to open and close doors for you and lead you in the direction He wants you to go.

DAY 17—WALK ON WATER

But seek first the kingdom of God, and His righteousness;
and all these things shall be added unto you.
Matthew 6:33 (KJV)

Yesterday I talked about giving over our futures to God. This is very difficult to do, because we want to know how things are going to end up for us. We often run through different scenarios of what could go wrong. What if this happens? What if that doesn't happen, etc.?

Other people can throw doubts and fears at us and make us second-guess what we are doing and where we are going.

God very clearly tells us to shut out those other voices and listen only to Him. When my mind starts spinning with thoughts of what-ifs, I am often reminded of the story of Peter walking on water. Jesus told him to look directly at Him and not look down or around at the waves and water surrounding him.

When Peter kept his eyes focused on Jesus, he did fine and was able to walk on water and do the impossible. But the moment he started focusing on what was going on around him, he started to fear and sink.

If you are being called to do something that goes against worldly logic, you will be challenged by outside influences and fears. Keep your eyes on Jesus and follow Him to wherever He is calling you. You will be safe.

Reflection:

Read Matthew 14:28-30. Ask God to show you any areas that you need to listen more to Him and less to the world.

DAY 18—WE WIN

Winning is fun, exciting, and energizing! Losing is deflating and discouraging. We have all had experiences with both of these extremes. At times, life feels like we are always running a bit behind, always fighting some sort of battle.

Society and the basic morality of the human race can easily discourage us in our Christian walk. It's hard to stand firm when everyone around you seems to be bending. But God wants us to be encouraged. He reminds us throughout the Bible that in the end, He wins! And it's important for us to consistently remind ourselves that as members of Christ's army, we win too! Philippians 3:14 (NLT) states, "I press on to reach the end of the race and receive the heavenly prize for which God, through Christ Jesus, is calling us."

There are days that I just feel tired—tired of trying, tired of fighting, tired of standing firm. I just want to quit going against the grain, and I want to join in with the world. But God calls us to stand firm, and He commands us to keep going.

When you feel defeated, go to His Word and be encouraged! We win! God does not promise us it will be easy. In fact, He warns us of the persecution we will face and the pressure to join in the worldly ways of life. "In this you greatly rejoice, though now for a little while, if necessary, you have been grieved by various trials," I Peter 1:6 (KJV).

However, God calls us to hold tight to Him and be encouraged. We win!

For the Lord your God is He who goes with you to fight for you
against your enemies, to give you the victory.
Deuteronomy 20:4 (ESV)

Reflection:

John 16:33 (NIV) states, "I have said these things to you, that in me you may have peace. In the world you will have tribulation. But take heart; I have overcome the world." Any time you feel discouraged, repeat this verse. You can also look up one of the many other verses God has given us to remind us of our victory (1 Corinthians 15:57, Romans 8:31, Romans 8:37, Philippians 4:13 and many others).

DAY 19—WHO MOVED?

"And, behold. I am with you always, to the end of the age."
Matthew 28:20 (ESV)

Every day, I drive by a church that has one of those billboards out front. I love seeing what the quote of the week is. I get excited about words. Being a writer, I love reading catchy little phrases, especially ones that pack a punch. Some of them stick with me, and some don't. One that has stuck with me for several years is the following:

If you're feeling far from God, guess who moved?

I'm not sure why this particular message has stuck with me for so long, but maybe it's because I can relate to it so well. I think we all feel far from God at times. We wonder why we can't feel His presence or why He is not answering a particular prayer we have.

Sometimes I feel let down by God. I can't sense His guidance or peace, and I feel like He is nowhere to be found.

Then I remember the billboard. If I really stop to think about it and am honest with myself, I can recognize where I've squeezed God out. I've gotten too busy to really hear Him, or I have my own ideas of what I want and am just waiting for Him to come along side me.

When we feel far from God, we need to stop. We need to look for where He is. He is still there, always. Look for Him and go back to where He is. Don't expect Him to run after you. He is waiting; He is patient. He will never leave us, but we often leave Him.

Reflection:

In Joshua 1:5 (NIV), God says, "I will never leave you nor forsake you." Whenever you feel far from God, pray and ask Him to show you where you veered off course.

DAY 20—OFFENSE

"It's easy to see a smudge on your neighbor's face and be oblivious to
the ugly sneer on your own. Do you have the nerve to say,
'Let me wash your face for you,' when your own face is distorted by
contempt? It's this I-know-better-than-you mentality again, playing a
holier-than-thou part instead of just living your own part. Wipe that
ugly sneer off your own face, and you might be fit
to offer a wash-cloth to your neighbor,"
Luke 6:41-42 (MSG).

Wow. Just sit and let that sink in for a minute. Do you have one or two circumstances that come to your mind when you stop and listen to God? I do. As a matter of fact, God brought this very scripture to me this morning after I prayed for direction over a situation at my home church.

I have been mightily struggling with forgiveness and acceptance over some very large direction-changes our church is making. I have several close friends who have been let go from their positions at the church due to these "changes in focus" that the church leaders have cited. Each of my friends has been very hurt over the dismissal.

I was an employee of the church for a period of time and worked very closely with each of these women, and I know their hearts were 100 percent in the right place.

I am struggling over the changes being made by the church leaders and have found myself struggling with the sins of offense and judgment. I actually walked out of the church service this past weekend, not able to stomach what I felt were the misleading reasons the church leaders gave the congregation for the many changes taking place.

I feel offended. I feel judgmental, and I feel angry. I don't know what to do with these feelings, but God is making it abundantly clear that I am not to sin in my anger. He brought me to the above passage in Luke 6 and also reminded me of a book I read a couple years ago called *The Bait of Satan.* It's an entire book about living free from the trap of offense.

Satan has a heyday when we judge other Christians, especially if it results in the falling apart of a church family.

I don't know what God will lead me to do as far as staying in our current church or finding another place to worship, but I do know one thing He is making clear, and that is to make sure I do not sin in my anger and I don't judge.

I know I don't have all the information. Only God does. I will follow my Father step-by-step and wait for His direction.

Reflection:

Is there an area of your life that you are struggling with offense or judgment? Ask God to reveal these to you. Read the book *The Bait of Satan,* by John Bevere if this is an area you struggle in.

DAY 21—BE A STONE

God needs you. Have you ever thought about that? You know God has a plan for you. You read that in Ephesians. But do you know that God's big, overall plan doesn't work without you? God called each and every one of us for a purpose. Your purpose is not the same as my purpose. He needs you to play a different role than He needs me to play.

Present yourselves as building stones for the construction of a
sanctuary vibrant with life, in which you'll serve as holy priests
offering Christ-approved lives up to God.
1 Peter 2:6 (MSG)

My husband just finished building a stone retaining wall in our backyard. Before it was built, we had piles upon piles of stones in our yard. None of the stones seemed extraordinary or special to me, but now they each have a very important purpose. If I were to use a pick to pull any one of the stones out of the retaining wall, the wall would become unstable and eventually crumble.

God's plan is like that, too. He needs each and every one of us to complete His project here on earth. So don't feel insignificant. You have a very important job to do. Be available to be a stone in God's sanctuary here on earth.

Reflection:

Read Luke 6. What are some of the jobs God has called you to do? Do these roles seem significant to you? Bring them before God and ask Him to impress your significance on you and show you ways to fulfill your purpose here on Earth.

DAY 22—LIGHT IT UP!

God is light, pure light;
there's not a trace of darkness in Him.
I John 1:5 (MSG)

I can be a news junkie. I have been known to sit for hours on end watching a news channel, even to the point where they start repeating newscasts. And, still, I watch.

There was one summer when I was following a very sad trial about a mother who was accused of murdering her young daughter and hiding her body in the woods. I was riveted by the story and followed it day in and day out.

I went through a significant depression that summer to the point that my husband was quite concerned for me and didn't know how to help me "snap out of it." At the time, I didn't, either.

Of course, there were other things going on at the same time. We were newly married and were going through the major adjustments of that. We were tight on money, so I was limited to what I could do to entertain two kids home from school all summer. And also just the daily stresses of living life here on Earth were present.

So it took me a while to put together why I was feeling so dark and down all the time. It took the trial ending and God's nudging clarity to figure out what my depression and hopelessness were caused by.

Now that I am aware of how watching too much bad news on TV can affect me, I have noticed that even political shows can have the same effect. Talk about darkness! Our country is changing its moral fibers rapidly, and it's not for the better.

I still follow news and politics to a degree, but I am careful not to saturate myself or my family in it. God is well aware of and predicted thousands of years ago that the world would get darker and darker over time. In some ways, we can actually take courage from it, because it means the time of Christ's return is nearing.

God tells us throughout His Word to be the light of the world. We are not to give in to the darkness or even be discouraged by it. We are to lean in to Christ's light, be the light for others and focus on God's hope, not on the world's hopelessness.

I John 1:7 (MSG) says, "But if we walk in the light, God Himself being the light, we also experience a shared life with one another, as the sacrificed blood of Jesus, God's son, purges all our sin."

Reflection:

I John 2:8 (MSG): *"The darkness is on its way out and the True Light already blazing."*

Remember, rejoice! We win! Look for God's continued light to give you hope and lead the way.

DAY 23—READILY AND CHEERFULLY

G od calls us to live positively. He wouldn't tell us to do something unless we could succeed in obeying Him.

Do everything readily and cheerfully—no bickering,
no second-guessing allowed! Go out into the world uncorrupted,
a breath of fresh air in this squalid and polluted society. Provide
people with a glimpse of good living and of the living God. Carry the
light-giving Message into the night so I'll have good cause to be proud
of you on the day that Christ returns. You'll be living proof that I
didn't go to all this work for nothing.
Philippians 2:14-16 (MSG)

Paul is telling us to get out there and brighten up the world! It's a choice we make daily: choose to let the darkness of the world dim our light or choose to be the light that the world can see shining through the darkness.

Sometimes this is really hard to do. There are days when I feel grumpy and irritable. I might feel judgmental toward other people or not have patience with those who make decisions I disagree with. I am definitely not shining God's light when I allow those negative emotions to take over. Sometimes I just feel overpowered by all the sin and pain that I encounter. God calls us to be His light to the world even when we are feeling overwhelmed. He doesn't expect us to do this on our own, however. He gives us the strength to rise above the darkness.

We have a job to do, and God has made it very clear.

Reflection:

Look for a way today to be a bright spot in our dark world. Smile at someone who seems angry or sad; bring grace when everyone else is bringing judgment; be honest when others are stretching the truth. Ask God to show you your opportunity today.

DAY 24—ATTITUDE IS EVERYTHING

You must have the same attitude that Christ Jesus had.
Philippians 2:5 (NLT)

Have you ever studied the life of Jesus? We can know all the Sunday school stories about Him: His birth, how He chose and called His disciples, when He fed the 5000 with very little bread and fish, His crucifixion and His resurrection. But how often do we really study Him, His attitude, His humility or His way of going to His Father for wisdom and guidance?

Can you imagine: the Son of God being humble? He was! And we are supposed to model our lives and our attitudes after Him.

God sent Jesus, His Son, to earth to die for our sins so that we might spend eternity in Heaven with our Creator. But God also sent His Son here to earth for a very different reason. Jesus walked this earth so that He would know our sorrows, know our temptations, and know our joys. And the beautiful thing about this is that through God's Word, we get to see how Jesus handled all of these earthly situations.

How did He react when people were angry with Him? What did He do when He was angry, sad or lonely? Jesus also showed us how to be joyful and celebrate.

He modeled how to be angry and yet not sin. He demonstrated how to go to the Father when we are sad or scared or feeling all alone.

We can learn so much about what God wants from us while we are yet on this earth by studying the life of Jesus.

Again, Jesus said, "Peace be with you!
As the Father has sent me, I am sending you."
John 20:21 (NIV)

Reflection:

Can you find a story about Jesus to which you can relate? (For example, Matthew 4, Matthew 23, Mark 3, 1 Thessalonians 4) How did Jesus handle His situation? How does He want you to handle yours?

DAY 25—THANK YOU!

I have gotten much better at remembering to bring things to God in prayer. When I don't know which way to go on a decision, I bring it to Him to show me. When I need help working through anger or judgment of others, I bring my emotions to God. When I need comfort, it's Christ I go to for help.

Once I've laid my troubles on the altar, I often feel lighter and can move forward with less angst.

I have recently realized that I often forget and neglect the next step. Many times, God's answers to our prayers come subtly and over time. It's often not a clear, all-of-a-sudden revelation He gives us or a clear-as-day discovery. God's ways are sometimes easy to miss. He works our anxiety out little by little over time, or He brings the comfort we asked for through unexpected and unrecognized means.

We must make a conscious effort to remember our petitions and to recognize God's hand in providing answers to them. One way to do this is to keep a prayer journal. Jot down the things you've placed before your Father and go back to it periodically to see which ones He has already answered.

Don't forget to thank Him for answered prayers, even if they were answered in a way you didn't see coming. You shouldn't have a one-way relationship with the Lord: asking for things but forgetting to thank Him when He resolves them for you.

Give thanks to the Lord, for He is good;
His love endures forever.
Psalm 118:1 (NIV)

Reflection:

Read Psalm 138. Remember to be thankful for the answers and blessings you have, not just focused on what you still want.

DAY 26—JOB SECURITY

Do you see what we've got? An unshakable kingdom.
And do you see how thankful we must be? Not only thankful,
but brimming with worship, deeply reverent before God. For God is
not an indifferent bystander. He's actively cleaning house,
torching all that needs to burn, and He won't quit until it's all
cleansed. God, Himself, is Fire!
Hebrews 12:28-29 (MSG)

D o you ever feel unimportant or like your life doesn't really matter in the big scheme of things? There are days when I feel as if I'm just spinning my wheels, putting one foot in front of the other. At times, it seems that no matter how hard I work, nothing really changes. Life feels meaningless, and I feel inconsequential. However, God has given us a purpose. We are to go into all the world, spreading the Good News. We matter to God and to His mission.

God is not an indifferent bystander, and neither should we be. We have work to do! God will not stop until it's over, and neither should we.

If that's not job security in a very important role, I don't know what is. You are part of God's plan; live like it!

But sanctify Christ as Lord in your hearts, always being ready to make a defense to everyone who asks you to give an account for the hope that is in you, yet with gentleness and reverence.
1 Peter 3:15 (NASB)

Reflection:

How are you partaking in God's work here on earth? Read Hebrews 12:1-3, and ask God to show you your role in His plan.

DAY 27—SUMMER BLUES

I get depressed in the summer. It's the strangest phenomenon. Most people start to feel down during the dark winter months. SAD, or Seasonal Affective Disorder, it's called. It's the opposite for me.

For some reason, my darkest times are in the bright, long, lazy days of summer. I don't know if it's the lack of a concrete schedule or if it's days on end without a break from raising children. I hate to admit it, but I am one of those moms who can't wait to send the kids back to school and get our family's structured schedule under way again. I actually love dark, cold, stormy winter nights where the only thing to do is curl up with a hot cup of tea and a good book.

I don't know why I'm like this. It's weird and strange and not at all what most people expect. But it's who I am; and I've chosen to accept it and work within this limitation of mine.

How do I get through these lonely, dark times? For one thing, I love myself through it. I pray. I write in my gratitude journal, and I accept. It's who I am. I treat myself in the summer like others need to treat themselves in the winter. I simply give myself a break. I lower the expectations I have of myself. I ask my husband and my children to give me a break. And I remind myself that this, too, shall pass.

I cling to God during these tough times, asking Him to give me peace and joy for the moment. The more I depend on Him, the more I can feel God's presence and am delivered.

Reflection:

Psalms 30:5 reminds us, "Weeping may endure for a night, but joy comes in the morning."

Give yourself a break and know that no matter how low you feel at any given time, it will pass. You will be rejoicing again soon.

DAY 28—SING

And sing, sing your hearts out to God! Let every detail in your lives-
words, actions, whatever-be done in the name of the Master, Jesus,
thanking God the Father every step of the way.
Colossians 3:16 (MSG)

God loves to hear our songs of praise. He calls us to sing to Him, to lift His name in song. This pleases Him greatly. It's one of the many ways we show our worship of Him.

But, do you also know that singing songs of praise to our Heavenly Father benefits us as well? It brings our focus back to God, turning our eyes and our hearts to Him over and over again.

Have you ever noticed that it actually feels good to sing? It not only feels great to turn our attention to our Perfect Father, but it also gives our lungs and vocal chords a mini massage.

Sometimes I just belt out a song while I am driving alone in my car. To my family's chagrin, sometimes I even do it when they are riding with me. It's especially fun when they start to sing along. None of us are good singers, and we sound horrible. But it's fun, and it pleases God.

Next time you sing aloud, notice the instant elevation of your mood as well as your body's well-being. Try it today. It's hard to be grumpy or depressed when you are singing praises.

Reflection:

Here is another version of Colossians 3:16 (NIV): "Let the Message of Christ dwell in you richly, as you teach and admonish one another with all wisdom through psalms, hymns and songs from the Spirit with gratitude in your hearts to God."

DAY 29—WHERE IS HE?

I'll let the lyrics of this Mandisa song speak for themselves:

Have you ever heard a love song that set your spirit free?
Have you ever watched a sunrise and felt you could not breathe?
What if it's Him? What if it's God speaking?
Have you ever cried a tear that you could not explain?
Have you ever met a stranger who already knew your name?
What if it's Him? What if it's God speaking?
Have you ever lost a loved one who you thought should still be here?
Do you know what it feels like to be tangled up in fear?
What if He's somehow involved? What if He's speaking through it all?
His ways are higher, His ways are best

Though sometimes strange
What could be stranger than God in a manger?
Who knows how He'll get a hold of us?
Get our attention to prove He's enough?
Who knows how He'll get a hold of you?
Get your attention to prove He's enough?
He'll do and He'll use whatever He wants to
To tell us "I love you"
God is speaking, "I love you"

97

Reflection:

Matthew 25:40 (NIV) The King will reply, "Truly I tell you, whatever you did for one of the least of these brothers and sisters of mine, you did for me."

Go out today and look for Him. Listen for Him. Ask Him to show Himself to you.

DAY 30—DECLAWED AND DEFANGED

Keep a cool head. Stay alert. The devil is poised to pounce,
and would like nothing better than to catch you napping.
Keep your guard up. You're not the only ones plunged into these hard
times. It's the same with Christians all over the world. So keep a firm
grip on the faith. The suffering won't last forever. It won't be long
before this generous God who has great plans for us in Christ-eternal
and glorious plans they are—will have you put together and on your
feet for good. He gets the last word, yes, He does.
1 Peter 5:8-11 (MSG)

We are warned many times throughout the Bible to be aware of and watchful for Satan's schemes. He knows our weaknesses. He watches for opportunities to strike and bring us down. He wants us to veer off the track God has set out for us. Sometimes I believe lies such as, "You'll never be able to succeed at that" or "You're not smart enough to do that." If I believe these lies of the enemy, I will stay stuck and feel oppressed.

Satan is portrayed in Scripture as a lion in wait for his prey, but in the reality of Christ, Satan is declawed and defanged. He can do no damage to you if you cling to Christ's freedom. 1 John 8:36 (TNIV) tells us, "So if the Son has sets you free, you will be free indeed." That's you! That's me! Praise God, and don't let Satan convince you otherwise!

It's up to each one of us to make the daily decision to seek Christ and be watchful for the devil's lies. Counteract the lies with God's Truth. 2 Corinthians 10:5 (ESV) says, "Take every thought captive to obey Christ."

Reflection:

What are your weaknesses? What lies does Satan use to keep you in bondage? Ask God to make you aware of your vulnerabilities. They are hard to admit and face sometimes, but knowing them is the only way to true freedom.

CONCLUSION

I have learned so much through the process of writing *Gratitude Greens*. I have had to rely on God's wisdom and direction when I felt that I had nothing more to say. I needed to rely on Him when doubts surfaced and my confidence dwindled. On grumpy, negative days, I had to pick myself up (with God's help) and practice what I preached.

It's been humbling, and it's been difficult at times. However, the main thing I am walking away with is a heart full of gratitude. I am so grateful that my Heavenly Father saw me through to the end. He is the One who pressed upon my heart the initial desire to write a book about gratitude. He gave me the concepts and words that He wanted me to share with the world. And He opened my eyes more and more to the importance of focusing on His light and His goodness and allowing myself to be used as His instrument.

I long to have God's light shine through me. I yearn to be used by my Savior to lead others to His love.

I pray that you, the reader, will let Christ shine His light through you as well. Use this book as a springboard for living a grateful and light-saturated life. The world desperately needs you, and so does the Father.

CONCLUDING VERSES

Your eyes are windows into your body. If you open your eyes wide in
wonder and belief, your body fills up with light. If you live squinty-
eyed in greed and distrust, your body is a dark cellar.
If you pull the blinds on your windows,
what a dark life you will have.
Matthew 6:22-23

Steep your life in God-reality,
God-initiative, God-provisions.
Matthew 6:33

Let the Word of Christ dwell in you richly as you teach and admonish
one another with all wisdom, and as you sing psalms,
hymns and spiritual songs with gratitude in your
hearts to God.
Colossians 3:16

And last, but definitely not least:

Oh! May the God of green hope fill you up with joy, fill you up with peace, so that your believing lives, filled with the life-giving energy of the Holy Spirit, will brim over with hope!

Romans 15:13

Stay grateful, and
GOD BLESS!

CPSIA information can be obtained
at www.ICGtesting.com
Printed in the USA
FFOW05n2126070414

9 780985 289614